# I Am NOT an Octopus

## an Octopus

### ANIMALS IN THE OCEAN

BY MARI BOLTE

PEBBLE
a capstone imprint

T0044765

Published by Pebble, an imprint of Capstone
1710 Roe Crest Drive, North Mankato, Minnesota 56003
capstonepub.com

Library of Congress Cataloging-in-Publication Data
Names: Bolte, Mari, author. Title: I am not an octopus : animals in the ocean / by Mari Bolte.
Description: North Mankato, Minnesota : Pebble, [2023] | Series: What animal am I? |
Audience: Ages 5-8 | Audience: Grades K-1 | Summary: "The ocean is salty and can be warm or cold. It covers 70 percent of the Earth and is my home. I love to hunt and eat fish but am not an octopus. I am a graceful swimmer and can jump out of the water but am not a dolphin. What animal am I? Use the clues and guess!"—Provided by publisher.
Identifiers: LCCN 2021060061 (print) | LCCN 2021060062 (ebook) | ISBN 9781666343434 (hardcover) | ISBN 9781666343472 (paperback) | ISBN 9781666343519 (pdf) | ISBN 9781666343595 (kindle edition) Subjects: LCSH: Marine animals—Juvenile literature. Classification: LCC QL122.2 .B65 2022 (print) | LCC QL122.2 (ebook) | DDC 591.77—dc23/eng/20211209
LC record available at https://lccn.loc.gov/2021060061
LC ebook record available at https://lccn.loc.gov/2021060062

Editorial Credits
Editor: Christianne Jones; Designer: Bobbie Nuytten; Media Researcher: Morgan Walters; Production Specialist: Polly Fisher

Image Credits
Shutterstock: Earth theater, 18, middle left 27, Irina Markova, (reef) Cover, Leonardo Gonzalez, 16, top right 27, Madelein Wolfaardt, 2, Mark Green, 22, bottom left 27, Matt9122, 6, top right 26, melissaf84, (eye) Cover, Natali Snailcat, (dolphins) design element, Ramon Carretero, 28, RayK Photos, 4, top left 26, Sergey Uryadnikov, 30Bottom of Form, Shpatak, 14, top left 27, slowmotiongli, 24, bottom right 27, StudioSmart, 8, middle left 26, Tory Kallman, 10, middle right 26, Vlasov_38RUS, (reef) design element, Vojce, 12, bottom right 26, Willyam Bradberry, 20, middle right 27

# Who Am I?

Oceans cover more than 70 percent of Earth's surface. It is where I live. Ocean water is salty. The water can be warm or very cold. Millions of plants and animals call Earth's oceans home.

But what animal am I? Read the clues to find out!

My skin helps me blend in with my surroundings. It helps me hide from predators and capture prey.

**But I am not an octopus.**

I have gills that let me breathe underwater. When I open my mouth, water flows over the gills. Then the gills take in the oxygen in the water.

**But I am not a grouper.**

Swimming sends water over my gills. I have to have my mouth open and swim at the same time to breathe. If I stop swimming, I can't breathe.

**But I am not a manta ray.**

I move from one place to another to mate and have babies. I can migrate thousands of miles.

**But I am not an albatross.**

My babies grow in eggs and hatch inside of me. After they hatch, they come out into the world.

**But I am not a seahorse.**

My sense of smell is amazing. I can sense a single drop of something in a huge amount of water.

**But I am not a salmon.**

I usually hunt for food alone. But sometimes, I hunt in a group. Schools of fish are easier to hunt and eat together.

**But I am not a sea lion.**

I have a tall fin on my back. It is called a dorsal fin. When I swim near the ocean's surface, it sticks out of the water. Some people think it is scary!

**But I am not a sailfish.**

I can be found in oceans around the world. Sometimes people see me near beaches. But I also explore the ocean's depths. I can dive thousands of feet deep to find prey.

**But I am not a sea turtle.**

A mouth full of sharp teeth means I have a powerful bite! Old teeth fall out and are replaced by new teeth.

**But I am not a piranha.**

I am a powerful hunter. I can swim more than 30 miles (48 kilometers) an hour when I hunt. I can even leap out of the water!

**But I am not a killer whale.**

# I am not an octopus

# or a grouper

# or a manta ray

# or an albatross

# or a seahorse

or a salmon

or a sea lion

or a sailfish

or a sea turtle

or a piranha

or a killer whale.

So what animal am I?

# I am a great white shark!

Speed, sharp teeth, and a good sense of smell make me a fearsome hunter. I can be found in every ocean in the world.

# COOL FACTS ABOUT
## SHARKS

There are more than 500 species of sharks around the world.

Greenland sharks are one of the longest-living animals on Earth. Sharks believed to be more than 250 years old have been studied.

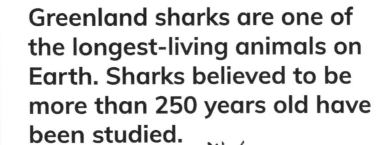

Shark fossils as old as 450 million years have been found.

Sharks are often called "living fossils." This means that they have not changed much over a long period of time.

Some sharks do not need to keep swimming to breathe. They have special cheek muscles that make this possible.

Some sharks migrate in search for warmer waters in the winter. Their food sources migrate at the same time. Sharks must follow their food if they want to eat.

# Books in This Series

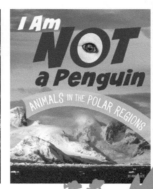

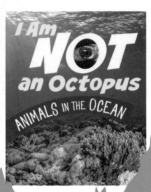

# Author Bio

Mari Bolte is an author and editor of children's books on all sorts of subjects, from graphic novels about science to art projects to hands-on history. She lives in southern Minnesota in the middle of a forest full of animals.